In this series –

RUMI READINGS
FOR
COMMUNICATION

RUMI READINGS
FOR
COMMUNICATION

JALALUDDIN RUMI

The Scheherazade Foundation CIC
85 Great Portland Street
London
W1W 7LT
United Kingdom
www.SF.Charity
info@SF.Charity

First published by The Scheherazade Foundation CIC, 2025

RUMI READINGS FOR COMMUNICATION

A CIP catalogue record for this title is available from the British Library.

ISBN 978-1-915311-77-1

Introduction

Jalaluddin Rumi was born in Balkh, Afghanistan, in the year 1207, and died in Konya, Turkey, in 1273.

During the sixty-six years spanning this pair of dates, he produced a range of extraordinary work in Persian which, today, is classed as 'Sufi Mysticism'.

In the seven and a half centuries since his death, Rumi's corpus, which includes *The Masnavi* and *Fihi Ma Fihi*, has been circulated widely across the Near East, the Arab world, and Central Asia.

Generations of students continue to commit selections of the 60,000 verses to heart, and allow Rumi's way of thought to permeate through all areas of their lives.

Although Orientalists venturing eastward from Europe in the 1700s occasionally made note of Sufi Mysticism, they tended to witness it through the more theatrical frills – such as 'whirling dervishes' – rather than through a deep appreciation of the texts.

It wasn't until the close of the nineteenth century that the first wholescale translations of Rumi's written work began to appear in Europe.

Even then, they remained very much the purview of a few academics, whose translations were – even for the time – laden with indescribably floral and cumbersome prose.

Although in the Occident, students would find themselves scrutinizing Rumi's corpus, it wasn't until more recently that accessible appreciations of his work became available.

A few years before his death, I asked my father – the Sufi scholar and thinker Idries Shah – for his thoughts on Rumi's legacy in the West.

Sitting in his favourite chair, a porcelain cup of green tea in hand, he looked at me hard.

'I never cease to be amazed,' he said.

'Amazed by what?'

'By the way people don't take what's perfectly packaged, and ready and waiting for them, but rather obsess with something else.'

'With what?'

'With endless and nonsensical trimmings, trappings, and paraphernalia.'

My father sipped his tea.

After a moment of silent thought, he continued:

'Read Rumi in the original Persian,' he said, 'and so delicate are the verses that you have tears rolling down your cheeks. Yet here in the West, it's served up as something submerged in a thick, glutinous gravy, so much so that its utterly inedible.'

I reminded my father that a series of publications had recently found their way to press – publications that presented Rumi's couplets in an utterly new way.

Stripped bare of what my father had referred to as 'gravy', they were light.

Indeed, they were lighter than light.

My father rolled his eyes at the thought.

'In any other place, and at any other time,' he said, 'people would be up in arms. Or, if they weren't, they'd be laughing until their sides split. Imagine it – Western poets with absolutely no knowledge of the original Persian text touting new, bestselling editions of Rumi's work! It's what we call "The Soup of the Soup of the Soup".'

In the years since my father's death, Occidental society has been flooded with all things Rumi.

Couplets ascribed to him are read solemnly at weddings across the United States, Europe, and beyond.

Wisdom drawn from his poetry is tattooed daily over the backs and limbs of Hollywood A-listers.

But the precious words uttered at weddings, tattooed into skin, and quoted in abundance, hold little or no bearing to the original verses of Jalaluddin Rumi.

So, there it is…

The great Sufi Master's wisdom available:

(a) in a form that's unreadable because it's all covered in glutinous gravy, or

(b) in another form that's completely distorted – the Soup of the Soup of the Soup.

One thing that *is* evident is that the West can benefit enormously from a clean, clear rendition of Rumi's thinking – as the East has done over the last seven hundred years.

For this reason, we have commissioned entirely new translations, gleaned in particular from *The Masnavi*. Selected and translated by native Persian-speaking scholars, the emphasis has been on maintaining the lightness of Rumi's poetry.

In an age of relentless speed and digital overload, and so as to allow the work to be accessed by those who may benefit from it most, we have arranged a series of bite-sized morsels by way of theme.

We encourage you to do what students, scholars, and ordinary people have done across the East for centuries...

To pick a single couplet, or a handful – and to read them over and over, allowing them to seed themselves in your mind.

Little by little, having taken root, they will blossom and bear fruit.

Tahir Shah

How to Use This Book

Rumi Readings for Communication

This book is about language – but not only spoken language.

It's about *connection*. About the invisible threads between people.

About the power of presence behind a word, a glance, a silence.

It is about what we say, and what we mean.

What we hide behind our speech – and what we reveal by accident.

Whether you're trying to become a better speaker, a more thoughtful listener, a clearer writer, or a more sincere human being, *Rumi Readings for Communication* is here to accompany you.

These verses, freshly translated from the original Persian texts by The Scheherazade Foundation, are arranged in ten themed parts. They explore speech, silence, trust, misunderstanding, nonverbal language, presence, and the subtle spiritual dimensions of expression.

In a time of constant messages, arguments, noise, and distraction – this book is a quiet place to recalibrate.

Not to teach you what to say, but to remind you how to listen.

More Than a Tool

Communication is often treated like a tool – a way to achieve something, persuade someone, get what we want.

But Rumi saw it differently.

He saw it as a spiritual act.
A mirror. A bridge. A form of love.
And also, sometimes, a cause of deep suffering when misused.

These quotes are not rules. They are *reflections*. They don't correct your grammar or fix your technique. They speak to the **inner posture** that makes real communication possible – honesty, humility, stillness, presence, clarity.

Let each quote settle into you slowly.
Let it show you something about how you speak – and how you listen.

A Book You Don't Have to Finish

This is not a book to 'complete'. It's a space to visit and revisit.

Some days you may read several quotes. Other days, one line is enough.

Keep the book close – on your desk, your nightstand, in your bag. Let it be a reference point in your day, especially when you feel misunderstood, unheard, or unsure of what to say.

You can follow the sequence, or open randomly. Trust that whatever you land on may hold something you need.

Ask Deeper Questions

After reading a quote, take a breath. Ask yourself:

- What is this revealing about how I communicate?
- Where am I quick to speak, but slow to listen?
- What kind of silence am I afraid of?

You might be surprised at what rises up. Let it be. Let the question do its work.

Let the Body Speak

Not all communication is verbal. In fact, much of it is not.

Rumi reminds us that a glance, a gesture, even a stillness, can carry meaning.

He speaks of scent and tone, of presence and absence, of the hidden message behind the words.

Let these quotes remind you to tune into more than sound.

To pay attention to the pauses.

To listen with your eyes.

To speak with your heart.

When Things Break Down

If you're in conflict, this book can help. If you're feeling isolated or unheard, let it meet you there. These quotes don't give easy answers – but they offer a deeper grounding.

A perspective that pulls you out of blame, out of panic, and back into presence.

Open to any page. Let the line be your anchor.
Let it ask something of you – not how to win, but how to connect.

Shared Language

You may find that a quote from this book is just what someone else needs to hear. A friend. A partner. A colleague. A student. A client. Don't be afraid to share it.

You can speak it aloud. Send it in a message.
Or simply hold it in your heart during a conversation.

Sometimes, even if you never quote it, it changes the way you speak.

Sometimes, it lets you say less – and be heard more.

Communication as a Mirror

How we speak reflects how we see the world. How we listen reflects how we value others. How we express ourselves reflects how we feel about being alive.

Rumi once wrote:
'The heart experiences peace through honest expression, as the thirsty find comfort in water.'

Let this book be a vessel of that peace.

Speak when it's time to speak.
Stay silent when silence is richer.
And return to these pages whenever your words – or your connections – need renewing.

Part 1
Effective Speech in Communicating

1

Like the nightingale's melodious song
among the blossoms
to capture their attention,
using the fragrance of the flower.

2

If you wish to speak words as sweet as honey,
exercise patience and refrain from indulging
in earthly delights.
Those who demonstrate patience
will achieve greater heights,
while those who indulge
will fall behind.

3

Avoid engaging in frivolous and baseless statements;
refrain from speaking with haughtiness and conceit.
Nonsense is but meaningless and ineffective words,
declarations and affirmations.

4

The heart experiences peace
through honest expression,
as the thirsty find comfort in water.

5

Imitators lack vitality in their language,
despite their self-justifications
and wide range of vocabulary.

6

When the speaker lacks vitality and substance,
who will show interest in their words
and their outcomes?

7

At that moment the true friend's words
were so profound and impactful
that they had the potential completely to disorient
and overwhelm you.
His mouth is a limitless source of wisdom,
like the infinite waters of the Euphrates.

8

A beggar who speaks words as valuable as gold
will not be able to sell his merchandise in the store,
since there is no market for it.

9

Reflect upon the ideal morsel
and the absolute lawful purpose;
since you are not flawless,
refrain from remaining silent.

10

The aroma of haughtiness,
the scent of greed,
and the fragrance of desire
permeate language
like the pungent smell of an onion.

Part 2
Skills for Effective Communication

11

To ensure articulate communication,
stay silent, and use words only sparingly.

12

As a newborn baby first drinks milk
then falls silent and focused on each syllable spoken to it,
so they must close their mouths
until they acquire the ability to communicate
by attentively listening to others speak.

13

O seeker,
your companion is your clarity of vision:
make sure it remains unclouded by dust and debris.
Be mindful;
speak in a manner that avoids harm or confusion;
refrain from letting unnecessary information
obscure your clarity.

14

Rustam,[1] brimming with trepidation and sorrow,
pressed onward.
Even the most nefarious encountered
an inner decay from overpowering dread.

---

1   Legendary hero in Persian mythology, protagonist of the *Shahnameh*.

15

Boldness often leads to recklessness,
diminishing the respect of others.
Heedlessness and forgetfulness breed wickedness,
consumed by profound reverence and admiration.

16

Unity does not stem from the abundance of physical entities;
consider the physical body as transient,
like a name carried away by the wind.
By contrast, a mouse lacks mental coherence,
reacting swiftly to the sound of a cat.

17

Given that the sun warms your back,
it is reasonable to expect courage from you.
What are the reasons for exercising caution?

18

Disregard his physical appearance or skin colour;
focus instead on his resolute mindset
and harmonious sound.
Regardless of his complexion,
he remains your source of harmony.
Acknowledge his shared humanity,
regardless of outward differences.

19

When you sincerely place your trust in someone,
this door of yours opens to numerous accomplishments.
A single coin becomes multiplied by four,
and one adversary transforms into a group of four.

20

Being in the company of friends places you
in a delightful and pleasant environment,
like being in a beautiful garden
filled with flowers.
By contrast, associating with enemies at this time
can lead to danger.

Part 3
Understanding the Elements
That Tarnish Relationships

21

Consuming the flesh of God's servants is prohibited,
and engaging in gossip will result in punishment.

22

An adversary is one who intends harm,
rather than inflicting harm upon himself.
A bat does not threaten the sun;
instead, it is its own enemy,
hiding in shadows.

23

Human beings may be compared to trees,
with their agreements like roots.
It is crucial to exert effort in nurturing
and caring for these roots.
A compromised agreement is like a decaying foundation,
devoid of its fruits and benefits.

24

Those people lack self-awareness,
indulging in slanderous speech about one another.

25

Henceforth, I shall disregard their murmuring,
as they merely echo the voices of evil spirits.
O heart, forsake them,
for they are mere empty shells.
Peel away their outer layers,
revealing nothingness within.
What is skin but a mosaic of words in various hues,
almost imperceptible,
like armour upon water.

26

As the gathering forms
among the Sheikh's discourse,
envy seeks to sow discord
among those consumed by jealousy.

27

Anger and lust divert an individual,
distorting their soul with relentless determination.
True art remains concealed
when its purpose becomes obscured.
Remove a hundred layers of obstacles
between the heart and the eye.

28

Those who exhibit excessive pride and resort to violence will neither receive divine forgiveness nor human love.

29

Do not weave webs of deception
and manipulation in your mind,
for success does not favour the crafty.

30

Avoid complacency with falsehood,
for neither water nor oil can extinguish its flame.

Part 4
The Quality of Nonverbal Communication

31

Beyond verbal and nonverbal expression,
a hundred thousand translators
spring forth from the depths of the soul.

32

O boaster,
your mournful appearance reveals the noxious smell
that emanates from your words.
Do not brag of your fabricated nimbleness;
advise the seasoned scent-detectives of life's battles.

33

My true colour is disclosed by my inner self,
not by my gilded face.

34

Your vital signs – pulse, complexion, and breath –
can reveal any ailments you are suffering.
These indicators – heartbeat, eyes, and skin tone –
enable the diagnosis of numerous illnesses.

35

Even if my outward demeanour seems bitter,
it is only that
my heart rejoices inwardly
by divine decree.
A parent's innocent gaze
shields their child from harm.

36

Distance or separation
often brings tears,
but there is also reunion,
and embracing loved ones.

37

When truth is illuminated by peace,
the heart does not rely on false words.

38

This witness, whether spoken or nonverbal,
reveals the hidden.
The essence of conflict is unveiled
through both words and actions;
both expose the secret and the mind.

39

As you observe an enemy's transgressions and sins,
you may find yourself gnashing your teeth.

40

Having forgotten the shape
he materialized,
a storm tore inside him.
His fists landed on his face
and head as he banged his skull
on the door and the wall.

Part 5

The Importance of Making a Connection

41

To know one's identity
on the Day of Judgement
is the essence of all knowledge.

42

However you present yourself,
you always claim,
'This is me,'
even if, by God's grace,
you are not that.
With this information as its cornerstone,
the manger can be supported
by the humble cow and sturdy camel.

43

A beggar in our midst stirs the wine,
and our minds spin the wheel.
It is we who become drunk,
not the wine itself;
it is we who give life to the form,
not the other way around.

44

There are many undiscovered rivers
that flow into your spirit,
whether you know it or not.
Your strength is a gift from the elements
which you can draw from both earth and sky.

45

The world supposedly revolves around a person's desires
when they become immortal.
The rivers and floods do as they like,
while the stars go where they want.
A leader's life and demise unfold in a linear fashion,
reflecting their desires.

46

The heart's function extended to shape the universe,
casting its essence into shadows.

47

One eye beholds two yards of scenery,
while another perceives the face of a king.
Dervishes transcend these distinctions,
where non-being merges with the highest sky.
Stop complaining about your woes,
for it guides the horse away
from the grasp of non-existence.

48

Since God is invisible,
prophets serve as His emissaries.

49

My faith lies in losing myself in the journey,
and my creed is in the non-existence within existence.

50

The Creator,
whose image you recognize,
manifests through the humanity of animals.

Part 6

The Benefits
of Self-Connection

51

As the spirit resides in secrecy,
the physical form is like a sleeve,
and mental faculties, a hand inside it.

52

How can blossoms turn into knots,
when flowers shine like armour?
Fruits emerge as blossoms fade;
even when the body weakens,
the spirit can still soar.

53

How can spring affect stones?
Transform into soil so a rainbow of blooms can emerge.
You have broken my heart for so long;
be down-to-earth for a change.

54

Disgrace befalls the king's prized falcon
accomplished in hunting partridges.

55

The struggle of the soul persists until death separates us.
Perfection is the only path to reaching the summit.

56

When it comes to the world around us,
the law of attraction dictates that
heat attracts heat, and cold draws cold.
Similarly, truthful individuals gravitate
towards others who value truth,
while deceitful individuals tend to
attract others of their kind.

57

Simply put, a friend's face is the mirror of the soul:
a reflection of who they truly are.

58

Examine your essence to discern its goodness;
this understanding underpins the core of religion.
By delving inward, you can better grasp
your personal identity,
your values and ideals as an individual.

59

As you seek solace within yourself,
you may notice imperfections in others.
Internally, harbouring animosity towards yourself
nurtures bitterness.
Externally, this bitterness is projected on to others.

60

A wise man was told by a beggar,
'No one here knows you.'
The sage replied,
'I know myself well; I know who I truly am.'
For he was aware of being an ordinary person.

Part 7
The Self

61

It transcends categorization, methodology, and moderation;
neither attached nor detached,
O Perfection.
By Your grace,
O admirable one,
we float in life's waters like fish.

62

He holds the shape and substance
of the universe of spirits, like a sea of innocence.
Behold this pristine ocean;
what imprint have you made on its shores?
Emerging from within,
waves observe one another.
He will make His worshippers cry out,
'Oh, beyond all limits!'
at the appointed time.

63

If this prayer should enrage You,
O Most High, show us the way to pray.
When the wicked demon expelled Adam from Paradise,
you allowed his return, rescuing him from the same fate.

64

A servant never raises their hands higher than You;
You are the source of prayer and its answer.
You grant the will to pray from the outset,
and You heed it till its end.
You are the beginning and the end;
we are the void in-between,
an emptiness beyond description.

65

O wise rescuer,
no one wills until You will it.
From You stem both the seeking
and the kindness.
Who are we to declare?
You are both the beginning and the end.

66

This prayer was Your command from the outset;
without it, dust would never have dared to act.
Marvellous, since You ordained us to pray,
we implore You to listen and respond to our prayers.

67

No one else seeks Him in this world;
no one else can satisfy a lover's longing for Him.

68

We were not, yet we were already cherished.
Even in silence,
God's grace listens.

69

Feel the love that ignites within this heart
for the Beloved when it strikes.
The more God's love permeates your essence,
the more certain it becomes that God loves you.

70

I am your senses, your pleasure, and your wrath,
He has proclaimed.
Depart from here, for apart from Me,
you perceive nothing.
You are more than a keeper of secrets;
You are the secret itself.

Part 8
God & Humans
in Relationships

71

No one looks anywhere but at the faceless;
    even the beloved has followed suit.
    While every dove has its religion,
      this particular bird is a sceptic.

72

All things, including the air we breathe
and the words uttered by magicians,
are part of God's creation.
Without uttering a single word,
God's allure communicates a hundred secret
meanings through cause and effect.

73

Just as menstruation allows exemption from prayer,
accepting Your call is a manifestation of Your mercy.
Blood mixes with prayer;
Your memory tarnishes like a simile and a donkey.

74

Essence, illusion, and attributes
do not define His concept of love.
Ignorance arises from limitations and traits;
it does not originate from You, Lord.

75

Mustafa[2] advised us,
'Do not engage in futile debates
about the essence of God.'

---

2   Another name for the Prophet Muhammad.

76

Remain on solid ground,
and do not venture into the depths of the ocean.
Stay content by the water's edge and speak sparingly.

77

He is like a fire,
and I am but a vessel;
I transform into whatever He wills me to be.
Whether a cup or a dagger,
I am as He creates me.

78

If seeking affirmation,
turn not away from the sun,
for it has arrived.

79

May mercy be upon you as I gently lead you,
for my joy lies in guiding you towards the unknown.
Also, reflect on other matters in the evening.
The ruler burnt the loaves of bread.

80

We emerge from the sea and return to it;
we ascend from the heights and journey upward.
One might say, '*Taa Allouah*,' a verse from the Qur'an.
The Mighty One fills us with awe.

Part 9

The Bond Between
Humans & Nature

81

There exists a fundamental connection
between soil, water, and flowers:
God infused life and emotion into each of them.

82

From a diet of soil, this very mouth has evolved,
yet the multicoloured earth –
everything here – the meat, the wine, and the sweets –
grounded in all sorts of patterns and colours,
O Dearest One!

83

Keep your portion sizes moderate,
avoid developing a habit of overeating,
and refrain from wasting food once you have
had enough.

84

When our essence itself is a creation of the heavens,
why do we feel compelled to cling
to this transient existence?

85

Once you glimpse the soul,
you will realize that this body is not your home.
Everything seen by humans
is confined to what the naked eye perceives.

86

O righteous ones,
this earth resembles a tree,
and we are its immature fruits.
Unfit for the palace in their raw state,
the unripe cling steadfastly to the branch.
Their grip loosens
as they ripen, acquiring a delightful flavour.

87

I became reliant on Your grace
as I was entrusted with that which the heavens declined.

88

From east to west,
the sky humbly serves His moon,
and all seek sustenance from Him.
His decree of '*Law lak*'[3] ensures
He sustains and distributes all.

---

3 A reference to the *Hadith*: 'Without you (O Muhammad) I would not have created creation.'

89

You have been submissive to the king
up to this point,
but from now on
you will command the arm.

90

Hundreds of thousands of sciences course through every
vein, taught to the father of humanity.
From the depths of his being,
he possessed the knowledge of every thing's true name.

Part 10
The Quality of Behaviour

91

Though you appear as a microcosm,
in your essence
you are the macrocosm.

92

Humans are not just inhabitants of the planet;
they constitute its very foundation.
While internally containing the seven heavens,
externally they can be swayed by the flutter
of a gnat's wings.

93

We are the echoes of our deeds,
and the universe is like a mountain
upon which they reverberate.

94

Fly like a bird in the field,
gaze ahead and behind,
as the grain sways this way and that.
The rhythm of breath, head, and face turns.
What a wonder!
With the intent to snatch this alluring prize from his grasp,
a hunter lurks both ahead and behind me.

95

The world serves both as a giver and a taker;
consider yourself a part of the latter.

96

Once more, humanity emerges from dust,
becoming the apex predator among its kind,
once sight and spirit part ways.

97

In the act of stealing, the thief is unaware;
his pursuers close in relentlessly.
Obsessed with possessions and locked doors,
he is blind to snares and the dawn's gentle sigh.
Consumed by greed, his focus is unwavering,
ignoring both the seeker and the searching.

98

Human senses endure beyond mortal bounds,
illuminated by the depth of the Day of Resurrection.
Light of sensation and eternal life intertwine;
unlike transient treasures, their brilliance will glow.
Those transcending worldly allurements
radiate with virtues and profound enrichments.

99

O wise and discerning servant,
do you grasp the true worth of your existence?
As precious as a gem unearthed from the depths,
your contribution is vital to every corner of the cosmos.

100

With this form acting as a calculator,
like the sun's light,
it symbolizes the spirit.

Finis